DEAR Dey

A Father's Letters of Christian Guidance and
Advice for a Joyful Marriage

Dr. Kola Alao, MD

This book is dedicated to my amazing wife, Queen Lola. Thank you for being not only an amazing mother but also my partner in this beautiful adventure of life. As Dey and Jeremiah embark on this new chapter, may your love and Godly guidance continue to inspire them just as they have inspired me.

Acknowledgement

From the moment you came into this world, you changed the rhythm of our lives. You arrived like sunlight after a long night—quietly at first, and then all at once, filling every corner of our hearts with warmth we had never known before. You have been our joy, our laughter, our hope, and the gentle reminder that love, in its purest form, lives in the simple miracle of a child becoming herself.

You are more than precious to me. You are the light that guided our family through years both beautiful and difficult. Your smile has softened hard days. Your laughter has lifted heavy hearts. And your presence—so genuine, so kind— has touched everyone fortunate enough to cross your path.

This book is a collection of memories, but more than that, it is a testimony. It is the story of watching a little girl grow into a remarkable woman. It is the story of every moment that shaped us as a family—moments of wonder, of struggle, of learning, and of love that deepened with every passing year.

Dear Dey

Dey, you have always been our sunshine. Not the kind that simply brightens a day, but the kind that brings life, warmth, and possibility wherever it shines. The world is gentler because you are in it.

On the day you begin a new chapter of your life, I offer you these pages not only as memories, but as a reminder: you have always been deeply loved, fiercely cherished, and endlessly believed in.

No matter where life carries you, no matter how many years pass, you will always be the little girl who made our world brighter simply by being in it.

With all the love a heart can hold,

Dad

Contents

Part Four: Understanding and Supporting Him   73

As you step into marriage, my heart is full of joy and gratitude. I have prayed for this day since you were a little girl, and now I watch you prepare to join your life with the man God has brought to you. Marriage is one of God's greatest gifts, but it is also one of His greatest responsibilities.

As both your father and a psychiatrist, I have walked with many couples through the joys and challenges of marriage. But more importantly, as a Christian, I believe God's Word holds timeless wisdom for building a marriage that not only lasts but thrives.

This book is not a list of rules but a collection of truths, insights, and prayers. It is my gift to you—guidance that blends God's Word with practical wisdom so you and your husband may build a home filled with love, joy, and peace.

I want you to remember this: Marriage is not about perfection. It is about growth, grace, and choosing each other every day. As you lean on God, you will find that He gives you the strength to love in ways beyond your natural ability.

Read these words slowly, return to them often, and let them remind you that you are never alone—your family, your faith, and your God are always with you.

With all my love,

Introduction

This book began as a private letter from me to my daughter on the eve of her marriage. I wrote it with a full heart—as a Christian, as a physician who has walked many couples through the complexities of relationships, and most deeply, as a dad who longs to bless his child with wisdom, encouragement, and truth.

Though these words were first intended for my daughter—whom I address fondly by names of endearment we have given her over the years—I believe they speak to something far larger than one family moment. Marriage is one of God's greatest gifts, and the questions, hopes, and challenges that surround it are shared by every couple who steps into that lifelong covenant.

Whether you are preparing for marriage, strengthening the one you have, or seeking to understand God's design for relationships, my prayer is that you will find something here that meets you where you are. These pages blend Scripture, clinical insight, and decades of walking with people through real-world joys and struggles. They offer not rules but reflections—not formulas but guidance rooted in faith, compassion, and lived experience.

And to the fathers who may read this, hoping to offer their own daughters guidance, I pray this book becomes a tool, a companion, and a voice alongside your own. May it help you speak blessing into your daughter's life, remind her of her worth, and encourage her toward a marriage shaped by grace, faith, and God's love.

You may not be my daughter, but you are someone's beloved child, created by God with purpose and dignity. My hope is that these words will speak to you as they spoke to her: with gentleness, clarity, and the steady reminder that God walks with you in every chapter of your life.

If you read with an open heart, I believe you will find encouragement, direction, and perhaps even healing within these pages.

Welcome, and may God bless you as you begin—or continue—the sacred journey of marriage.

How to Use This Book

This book is a collection of lessons, memories, and prayers from my heart to yours as you enter this new season of marriage. Each chapter contains a truth I wish I had fully understood earlier in my life—truths I now want to pass on to you.

You'll notice that every chapter follows a pattern and contains the following:

- **A Verse:** a foundation from God's Word

- **Insight:** a practical truth for life and marriage. This often includes a personal reflection, a story or wisdom from our life together

- **Tips:** practical ways to live out the lesson

- **Red Flags:** warning signs that something may be out of balance

- **Reflection:** a chance for you to pause, think, and apply the lesson personally

- **Prayer:** a blessing spoken over you and Jeremiah

Dear Dey

My hope is that this will not just be a book you read once, but it will be a companion you can return to again and again as you and Jeremiah grow together.

Part One:

Preparing for a Godly Marriage

1

Pursue God First—He Is Your True Anchor

Seek first the kingdom of God and His righteousness, and all these things shall be added to you. (Matthew 6:33)

Insight

Placing God first anchors every other area of life, including marriage.

I wish I had learned this earlier in my life. I spent much of my youth pursuing academics and achievements. Though I was saved at the age of ten, I did not make pursuing God my first priority. But God, who created us, does not tolerate being placed second to anything or anyone.

Dey, in your marriage, remember this truth: Jeremiah is a gift from God, but he is not your god. If you keep God first, everything else will fall into its rightful place.

When your anchor is Christ, no storm in marriage will be able to shake you beyond repair.

Tips:

1. Start and end each day with God through prayer, worship, or Scripture.
2. Attend church together consistently, and serve as a couple.
3. Seek God's wisdom before making major decisions in your marriage.

Red Flags:

1. If you find yourself consistently too busy for prayer or Scripture, you may be drifting from your anchor.
2. If conflicts with Jeremiah cause you to withdraw from God instead of drawing closer, it's a sign to realign your heart.
3. If you're making big decisions without praying first, pause and bring God back to the center.
4. If you feel emptiness, even when things are going well, check to see whether God still holds first place in your priorities.

Reflection:

1. What does it look like for you to practically "seek God first" in your daily life?
2. When have you felt most anchored in God's presence?

3. What distractions tend to compete with your time and devotion to Him?

4. How can you and Jeremiah help one another keep God first?

Prayer:

> *Father, may Dey always seek You first in every season of her life and marriage. Let her anchor be in You so that storms will not overwhelm her and blessings will not distract her. In Jesus Christ's name. Amen.*

2

Invest in Yourself—Never Stop Growing

Strength and dignity are her clothing.
(Proverbs 31:25a ESV)

Insight

Ongoing personal growth prevents stagnation and burnout.

Dey, do you remember how you used to tell me, "I don't live to work; I work to live"? You have always valued rest, relaxation, and experiences over simply grinding through life. Do you remember how you insisted on pre-engagement counseling before moving forward with Jeremiah? That wisdom has already built a strong foundation for your marriage.

Please continue to nurture that spirit of growth. Don't stop learning, don't stop exploring, and don't stop feeding your mind and soul. You have taught me so much about personal growth and development. You were the one who inspired your mom and me to write our first books. In fact, you believed in me at times when I struggled to believe in myself.

I smile when I picture you on a beach or in a hammock with a book in hand. Don't ever stop reading. From the time you were a child, your talents were obvious—you excelled in every subject and consistently made the honor roll. You chose occupational therapy instead of physical therapy because you wanted a career with broader options and diverse opportunities. That was a wise and forward-thinking decision.

You've already made it to forty-nine out of the fifty states—what a testament to your adventurous spirit! Keep going. Don't let your growth or curiosity slow down. Continue to fill your life with new experiences, knowledge, and creativity.

Tips:

1. Keep hobbies, friendships, and learning alive. Continue your travels.

2. Practice self-care so you can give from a full heart.

3. Set aside intentional "growth time" each week—whether it's reading, journaling, attending a workshop, or listening to a podcast that stretches your perspective.

4. Keep your marriage fresh by learning new things together—take a cooking class, learn a new sport, or plan trips that will challenge both of you.

5. Surround yourself with people who inspire and challenge you to become your best self.

Red Flags:

1. If you haven't traveled, explored, or done something new in months, you may be neglecting your adventurous side.

2. If you haven't read, journaled, or fed your mind in a while, it could be a sign of burnout or disconnection.

3. If you find yourself giving and giving but feeling empty, it may mean you are neglecting self-care.

4. If your days feel repetitive and uninspired, that's a sign that you need to make intentional space for growth again.

5. If you stop dreaming about the future or setting new goals, ask God to reignite your passion.

Reflection:

1. What new skill, hobby, or experience would you like to pursue this year?

2. How can you and Jeremiah intentionally grow together as a couple?

3. When was the last time you felt truly inspired by a book, trip, or conversation? How can you create more moments like that?

4. Are there any areas of your life right now that feel stagnant? What small step could you take this week to bring renewal?

Prayer:

Father, I pray that Dey and Jeremiah will never stop growing—in wisdom, in love, and in joy. May they always be curious, always be learning, and always encourage each other to become the best version of themselves. Let their marriage be a garden where new experiences, knowledge, and love blossom daily. In Jesus Christ's name. Amen.

3

Build Your Identity in Christ Before Marriage

Christ lives in me.
(Galatians 2:20 paraphrase)

Insight

Rooted identity prevents unhealthy dependence on a spouse. Your spouse complements you, but he does not define you.

Your identity is who you are—not what someone calls you, labels you, or tries to make you.

Dey, I'll never forget the day I was upset with you and jokingly said I would get another daughter. Without hesitation, you confidently replied, "I cannot be replaced." That moment showed me how deeply you understood your value as my daughter.

In the same way, I don't need to remind you of your identity in Christ—you already know it. Marriage does not erase or redefine that identity. Your DNA as a child of God will never change. There may be moments in marriage when circumstances or emotions cause you to question yourself, but please remember that you are Adeyoola Alao. You are not only a natural princess but also God's possession—chosen, loved, and called by Him before you were even born.

Nothing, absolutely nothing, can separate you from the love God has for you or from the love I have for you as your father.

Tips:

1. Remind yourself daily of your identity and who you are in Christ.

2. Don't expect your husband to meet every emotional need—he cannot, just as you cannot meet all of his needs. Only God can fill the deepest spaces.

3. Keep personal time with God at the center of your life, even after marriage.

4. Speak affirmations of truth over yourself when doubts arise.

Red Flags:

1. If you find yourself constantly needing Jeremiah's approval to feel secure, pause and realign your heart with Christ.

2. If you begin to lose sight of your passions, values, or calling, it may be a sign that you are leaning too much on another person for your sense of worth.

3. If disagreements or disappointments in marriage make you question your identity, remember that conflict does not define who you are—Christ does.

4. If you catch yourself comparing your life or marriage to others, stop and remind yourself of God's unique plan for you. Comparison is a thief of joy and identity.

Reflection:

1. When have you felt most confident in your identity in Christ?

2. Are there areas of your life in which you are tempted to seek approval from others instead of God?

3. How can you and Jeremiah encourage one another to stay rooted in your God-given identity?

4. What truth from Scripture can you hold onto when doubts about your worth arise?

Prayer:

Father, I pray that Dey's identity will always remain firmly rooted in You. May she never forget that she is chosen, loved, and irreplaceable in Your eyes. As she walks through marriage, let her security and confidence come from Christ alone so that she and Jeremiah can love one another from a place of wholeness. In Jesus Christ's name. Amen.

4

Invite God into Your Home— Pray as a Couple

For where two or three gather in my name,
there am I with them. (Matthew 18:20 NIV)

Insight

Couples who pray together often experience deeper unity, quicker forgiveness, and greater peace in their relationship.

Dey, I want to share something important about prayer. You may remember Peter Scazzero's book, *Emotionally Healthy Spirituality*. In it, he talks about the practice of the "daily office," a rhythm that some monks observed—pausing to pray and connect with God several times a day rather than relying only on one long prayer in the morning or at night. I would love for you to continue this kind of spiritual rhythm in your own life. Even more, I encourage you to invite Jeremiah into it with you.

The Bible tells us that one can put a thousand to flight, but two can put ten thousand to flight (Deuteronomy 32:30). Prayer multiplies in power when done together with others. I remember when we were in Alaska—you wanted to see a moose, but we hadn't seen one the whole trip. On the last day, you asked me to join my faith with yours, and we prayed. To our amazement, on the way to the airport, we finally saw a moose! That moment was a reminder that when we join our faith and prayers together, God listens and moves.

Dey, never forget that you and Jeremiah are stronger together than apart. Make prayer a habit—not just for yourself but for your marriage.

Tips:

1. End each day with a short prayer together, even if it's only for two minutes.
2. Pray over both big and small decisions as a team—whether it's buying a house, planning your future, or choosing how to spend your time.

Red Flags:

1. Not setting a regular time for prayer can lead to neglecting it altogether.
2. Unresolved conflicts might create tension, making it difficult to pray together.

3. Allowing distractions from technology or social commitments can disrupt your prayer time and focus.

Reflection:

What is one area of your marriage right now that you can begin praying about daily with Jeremiah?

Prayer:

> *Father, thank You for the gift of prayer and the strength it brings when we come before You together. Teach us to seek You in both small and big matters, and let our unity in prayer draw us closer to each other and to You. In Jesus Christ's name. Amen.*

Part Two:

Nurturing Your Relationship

5

Make Your Husband Your Partner (After God)

Therefore a man shall leave his father and
mother and be joined to his wife, and they
shall become one flesh. (Genesis 2:24)

Insight

Loyalty to your spouse shuts the door to outside interference. Even small cracks can become entry points for the enemy, so guard your unity.

Dey, many people miss this truth. It is natural to feel strong attachments to parents, siblings, and relatives. But the Word of God is clear: leave and cleave (Genesis 2:24). Many marriages run into difficulties because couples fail to fully embrace this principle.

One of the strongest examples is the bond between fathers and their daughters or between mothers and their sons. These are beautiful relationships, but once you are

35

married, your first earthly priority shifts to your husband. That doesn't mean you cut off your family or ignore your friends, but your loyalty and partnership now belong first to your spouse.

Ideally, your friends should naturally become his friends, and his should become yours. Still, it is healthy for both of you to have individual friendships. There are some struggles women understand better than men and vice versa. The important thing is that no friendship or family tie should come before your marriage.

The only exception to this principle is in cases of abuse or controlling behavior—but as we have prayed, that will not be your portion.

Tips:

1. Never prioritize family or friends above your husband.

2. Share your joys and struggles with him before you share them with anyone else.

Red Flags:

1. If you find yourselves overlooking each other's emotional and spiritual needs, it can lead to feelings of distance and resentment in your relationship.

2. If you notice that one of you is consistently putting work, friends, or personal interests ahead of nurturing your relationship, it may weaken your bond.

3. If you observe that you're not actively encouraging each other's spiritual development, it can diminish your connection.

Reflection:

1. Are there areas in your life in which you still rely more on family or friends than on your husband?

2. How can you intentionally build unity and partnership with him in your daily life?

3. Are you careful to guard your marriage from outside interference, even in small ways?

Prayer:

Father, help Dey to always honor her husband as her closest earthly partner. Give them the grace to be united in spirit, loyal to each other, and protected from outside interference. May their bond grow stronger each day as they walk with You. In Jesus Christ's name. Amen.

6

Establish Healthy Boundaries with Family and Friends

Above all else, guard your heart, for
everything you do flows from it. (Proverbs 4:23 NIV)

Insight

Boundaries are not walls; they are gates that protect intimacy from intrusion.

Dey, you once helped me write about boundaries in my book, *What I Wished I'd Learned.* Now I want you to carry those same principles into your marriage. Marriage is a gift from God, and because it is so beautiful, the enemy will often try to disrupt it. One of the greatest protections God has given us is the wisdom to set healthy boundaries.

I remember when your mom and I used to call you right after communion every Sunday. We never wanted the conversation to end, so we would reach out again. One evening, you didn't pick up the phone. At first, it felt unusual, but later I realized what you were doing: You were setting boundaries. You valued peace after communion, and once you communicated that, we adjusted. It was not rejection; it was wisdom.

Dey, you are an extrovert, always full of energy, kindness, and generosity. You love people, and you often sacrifice for them. But remember that you don't need to set yourself on fire to keep others warm. Healthy boundaries will help you protect your marriage, your peace, and your walk with God. Apply them wisely with your parents, siblings, friends, and in-laws.

Tips:

1. As a couple, decide how much influence your parents, friends, and in-laws should have in your marriage.

2. Protect your personal "me time" and "us time" from constant outside demands.

3. Don't be afraid to lovingly say *no* when necessary—it creates space for a healthy *yes.*

Red Flags:

1. Constant pressure to attend events or fulfill requests may indicate unclear boundaries leading to potential burnout.

2. When family or friends frequently interfere in your personal choices, it may show a lack of respect for your autonomy.

3. If you feel that your personal space or private matters are being scrutinized, it may suggest that your boundaries are not being honored.

4. Patterns of guilt-tripping or shaming for setting limits indicate serious boundary issues that can harm your emotional well-being.

Reflection:

1. Boundaries may sometimes feel uncomfortable, especially with those we love, but they are necessary for growth. Dey, remember that when you honor your marriage covenant, you are also honoring God. True love knows when to step back so what matters most can flourish.

Prayer:

Father, thank You for the gift of relationships and the beauty of marriage. Give Dey and her husband wisdom to set healthy, loving boundaries that will protect their peace and deepen their intimacy with You and with each other. Help them to walk in kindness without compromise and to guard their hearts with wisdom. In Jesus Christ's name. Amen.

7

Respect—The Language of a Husband's Heart

Submitting to one another in the fear of God.
(Ephesians 5:21)

Insight

Respect reaches a man's heart in a way nothing else can. Contempt, on the other hand, is not a fruit of the Spirit.

Dey, the Bible in Ephesians 5:33 teaches, "Each one of you also must love his wife as he loves himself, and the wife must respect her husband" (NIV). The apostle Paul also set the standard extremely high for husbands in Ephesians 5:25, saying, "Husbands, love your wives, just as Christ loved the church and gave Himself for her." That is a near-impossible task, and yet it is what God calls men to do.

My take is this: A man responds more deeply to being respected than to being loved, just as women often respond more to being loved than to being respected. I have watched you show tremendous respect for Jeremiah, and I have also seen how positively he responds to it. Please keep this up.

There will be times when he may not act in a way you think deserves respect—respect him anyway. And don't just show respect when he is present; do the same when he is not around. Speak about him fondly whether or not he is there to hear it. You are already doing this beautifully.

I remember when we went to the New York State Fair a few years ago. There was a pull-up challenge, and you confidently told the attendant, "My dad can do fifty pull-ups if he wants to." You may not have realized it, but that single statement touched a place in my heart that is hard to describe. Your confidence in me lifted my spirit so much that if you had asked me for $1,000 that day, I would have written the check without thinking! That is the power of respect.

Dey, do the same for Jeremiah—your respect will fuel his strength in ways you may never fully see. This is different from the way you motivated me when you were five years old. You once looked at a picture of me when I was younger and said, "Dad, I didn't know you used to be thin." It was like a dagger to my ego, but it became the motivation I needed to lose nearly 100 pounds. It was an innocent observation but incredibly effective. Your words carried weight then, and they will carry even greater weight in your marriage.

Tips:

1. Use affirming words daily—encouragement is like oxygen for a man's soul.
2. Disagree in private, not in public—protect his dignity as you would want him to protect yours.

Red Flags:

1. There should be **zero tolerance** for any emotional, physical, mental, or spiritual abuse toward you from anyone. Absolutely no exceptions.
2. Be cautious about spending time with people who habitually disrespect their spouse. Their words and attitudes can subtly influence your own.
3. If conversations with friends or family turn into spouse-bashing sessions, redirect the discussion or step away.
4. Guard your heart against comparison. What you feed your mind will eventually shape your attitude toward Jeremiah.

Reflection:

Respect is not about perfection—it is about choice. Even when Jeremiah falls short, your consistent respect will remind him of the man God is shaping him to be.

Just as your words once lifted me, your words will continue to lift him.

Prayer:

Father, thank You for the gift of respect and for the way it strengthens the bond of marriage. Help Dey to continually honor Jeremiah with her words, attitudes, and actions. Give her wisdom to show respect, even in difficult moments, and grace to build him up as the man You are calling him to be. In Jesus Christ's name. Amen.

8

Show Love in the Way He Understands

Let us not love with words or speech but with
actions and in truth. (1John 3:18 NIV)

Insight

Meeting your husband's emotional needs in his unique love language builds deep trust and security in your marriage.

Sunshine, quality time and acts of service are your primary love languages. I know this because you made me read Dr. Gary Chapman's book, *The Five Love Languages*, and even take the quiz! But you didn't stop there—you study people carefully and adjust how you show love to meet their needs. I remember when you were in the 9th grade and it was hard to buy me a gift. Instead of giving up, you researched the kinds of live music I enjoy and surprised me with a concert. You didn't even like jazz, but you went with me anyway just so I could have fun. That is a picture of your selfless heart, a true reflection of the way God made you.

Tips:

1. Discover his top two love languages.

2. Practice them intentionally every week, not just when it is convenient.

Red Flags:

Use Gary Chapman's love language test, and watch for the following as appropriate:

1. Touch: Minimal physical affection can leave your spouse feeling unloved, especially if you both value touch as a love language.

2. A noticeable absence of dedicated time together may lead to feelings of neglect, particularly if you both appreciate quality time.

3. Overlooking each other's effort to help can diminish the sense of being valued, especially if acts of service resonate with you both.

4. A lack of compliments or encouragement can lead to feeling unappreciated, particularly if verbal affirmations are important to you both.

5. Little interest in each other's passions may create emotional distance, especially if sharing interests is crucial.

6. Failing to recognize each other's emotional needs during tough times can lead to feelings of isolation, especially when you both need emotional support.

Additionally, it's important to note that his love language may change over time, so regularly studying and discussing these needs is essential for maintaining a strong connection.

Reflection:

1. Are there times when you've expected him to love you in *your* language without considering his?

Prayer:

> *Father, teach Dey to love not only in words, but in ways that truly reach her husband's heart. Help her to recognize and honor the love language You wired into him so their marriage may reflect Your sacrificial love. In Jesus Christ's name. Amen.*

9

Be His Greatest Encourager and Cheerleader

And let us consider how we may spur one
another on toward love and good deeds.
(Hebrews 10:24 NIV)

Insight

Consistent encouragement boosts motivation and builds deep confidence in your husband's God-given calling.

Tamilore, I don't think you need me to remind you of this because you are a natural encourager. The way you inspired me, gave me confidence, and believed in me while I was writing my first book is just one example of how God has blessed you with the gifts of exhortation and edification. You have a way of seeing potential in others and calling it out.

Sometimes you may catch a vision that Jeremiah does not see. In those moments, motivate him gently. I remember when we were in New York City and Uber had just started. I wanted us to take a taxi to JFK, but you insisted we try Uber instead. You stood your ground respectfully yet firmly, and you were right—it worked out beautifully. In the same way, there will be times in your marriage when you will see possibilities that Jeremiah may overlook. Encourage him, affirm his strengths, and gently redirect him when God shows you something he has not yet seen.

Remember, encouragement is not just about words but also about presence. Your steady belief in Jeremiah will become a shield for him when life brings challenges.

Tips:

1. Speak life over his efforts even when results are still unfolding.
2. Celebrate progress, not just outcomes—remind him that small steps matter.
3. Be quick to affirm his strengths in public, but offer correction in private.

Red Flags:

1. Regularly pointing out flaws or shortcomings without acknowledging his strengths can undermine his confidence.

2. Failing to recognize or celebrate his achievements, big or small, may leave him feeling unappreciated.

3. Not showing interest in his passions or activities might indicate emotional distance and a lack of support.

4. Frequently comparing him unfavorably to others can diminish his self-worth and discourage him.

Reflection:

1. How do you currently encourage Jeremiah in his daily life?

2. Are there areas in which he needs more affirmation and support from you?

3. How can you gently redirect him without discouraging or criticizing him?

Prayer:

Father, help Dey to be a faithful encourager to her husband. Teach her to use her words and actions to strengthen his heart, to believe in his calling, and to celebrate his victories both big and small. May her encouragement always point him back to You as the true source of his strength. In Jesus Christ's name. Amen.

Part Three:

Communication and Conflict

10

Speak Clearly—He Can't Read Your Mind!

A gentle answer turns away wrath, but a harsh
word stirs up anger. (Proverbs 15:1 NIV)

Insight

Clear and gracious communication prevents misunderstanding, builds intimacy, and protects your marriage from unnecessary conflict.

Tamilore, one of your God-given gifts is your excellence in communication. You are a compassionate listener and have a unique ability to see the perspective of others. Honestly, I should be the one taking lessons from you.

Do you remember the car wash incident when the Lord showed me that I needed to learn from you? We had gone through the car wash twice that day. The first time, while the attendant was telling us about an upgraded service we could purchase, I was impatient with him and cut him off to say we just wanted the basic wash. Later that day when we had to get a second car wash, the same attendant was there and you graciously listened to his sales pitch before telling him we wanted to stick with the basic wash. Right then, the Holy Spirit convicted me about my earlier impatience that I not only apologized to you, but also to the attendant. That moment revealed how deeply God has equipped you in this area.

The Word of God reminds us to be quick to listen, slow to speak, and slow to become angry (James 1:19). This does not mean that you should hold back your thoughts or silence your convictions. Rather, this verse encourages you to continue advocating for your views with the same grace and gentleness that you've always shown, even teaching me along the way.

When it comes to communicating with Jeremiah, remember to be clear and concise. Men, in general, are not as naturally perceptive as women. They often require more direct and straightforward communication. If there is something important you want to discuss, find a time that works best for him—preferably not when he's tired or hungry ("hangry"). As you both mature and go through different seasons of life, you will need to adapt your communication style to meet the changing needs of your marriage.

Tips:

1. Express your needs directly, not indirectly—don't assume he knows what you are thinking.

2. Use "I feel" statements instead of "You did this" to avoid sounding accusatory.

3. Choose the right time and setting for serious conversations. Timing matters.

4. Remember that tone carries as much weight as words, and gentleness disarms conflict.

Red Flags:

1. Using unclear language or ambiguous phrases can lead to misunderstandings about your feelings or needs.

2. Frequently sidestepping important discussions can leave him confused about your thoughts and emotions.

3. Relying solely on body language or facial expressions without verbalizing your feelings may create confusion.

4. Expecting him to understand your feelings or needs without expressing them can create emotional distance.

Reflection:

1. Do you sometimes expect Jeremiah to "just know" what you need without telling him?

2. How can you practice being both clear and gentle when expressing your thoughts?

3. What communication habits have you developed that need to be strengthened—or changed—for the good of your marriage?

Prayer:

> *Father, give Dey wisdom to communicate with love, patience, and clarity. Help her to listen well and speak in ways that build up her husband instead of tearing him down. Guard her tone and timing, and remind her that her words carry the power of life. In Jesus Christ's name. Amen.*

11

Resolve Conflict with Grace— Apologize Quickly

If it is possible, as far as it depends on you,
live at peace with everyone.
(Romans 12:18 NIV)

Insight

Peace in marriage is not nurtured by avoiding conflict but by resolving it quickly with humility, honesty, and forgiveness.

Alake, conflict is inevitable in marriage. What matters most is not how often disagreements happen but how you and Jeremiah choose to resolve them. The Bible encourages us to live at peace with everyone. Peace doesn't mean avoiding hard conversations—it means handling them with maturity, humility, and grace.

You have confronted me on a few occasions when I made poor decisions. You were always polite but firm. One unforgettable example of how *not* to resolve conflict was when you took the key to my car so I wouldn't go to work. You were trying to express your frustration about the fact that I was working too much. While the action itself wasn't the best approach, your motive was love and concern. I also admire how, when you want to have a difficult conversation, you often ask me if I am ready for it. That shows sensitivity to my emotional state in that moment—a practice I encourage you to continue with Jeremiah.

When emotions run high, sometimes the wisest choice is to pause, breathe, and take a short break before continuing the discussion. This prevents saying words in anger that can wound deeply. Always remember that the goal is not to "win" an argument but to strengthen the relationship and find solutions together.

A powerful part of resolving conflict is learning to apologize quickly. James reminds us:

> Confess your sins to each other and pray
> for each other so that you may be healed.
> (James 5:16 NIV)

Saying "I was wrong" without making excuses is one of the most healing phrases in marriage. But apologies must go hand in hand with changed behavior to demonstrate sincerity and commitment to growth.

Your encouragement, humility, and quickness to own your mistakes will create a safe space where Jeremiah can also be vulnerable. This cycle of grace and forgiveness will build resilience in your marriage and protect it from bitterness.

Tips:

1. Take breaks when emotions run high—return when calm.

2. Focus on solutions, not victory. Don't dwell too long on the conflict itself.

3. Say "I was wrong" without excuses or blame-shifting.

4. Follow every apology with action that proves sincerity.

Red Flags:

1. Withdrawing from conversation or giving the silent treatment may indicate a refusal to engage and address the issue at hand.

2. Bringing up past conflicts during new disagreements can demonstrate an inability to move forward and resolve issues.

Reflection:

1. How do you usually react when conflict arises? Do you withdraw, get defensive, or seek peace?

2. Are you quick to apologize, or do you delay out of pride?

3. How can you create an atmosphere in which Jeremiah feels safe to admit his mistakes too?

Prayer:

Father, help Dey to handle conflict in her marriage with grace and humility. Teach her to pause before speaking in anger, to apologize quickly when she is wrong, and to seek solutions instead of winning arguments. May their home be filled with peace, forgiveness, and Your healing love. In Jesus Christ's name. Amen.

12

Pick Your Battles—It's Not a War

A person's wisdom yields patience; it is to
one's glory to overlook an offense.
(Proverbs 19:11 NIV)

Insight

Emotional regulation and discernment prevent unnecessary escalation and protect intimacy in marriage.

Mojoyinola, one of the mistakes I have made in life was fighting unnecessary battles. This is an area in which I don't think you need much advice because God has already given you wisdom in this. Still, I will include it because it is important in marriage.

It is not worth fighting over little things. It is okay to let some things slide as long as they are not crucial, sinful, or against your values and biblical principles. I have never seen you pick unnecessary fights or quarrels. In fact, you have often shown longsuffering and patience.

I remember when you were about fifteen, and we were at JFK waiting to board our flight to Syracuse. We watched a teenager being rude to her father. I was about to confront the father for allowing his daughter to behave that way, but you looked at me and simply said, "Dad." That one word stopped me in my tracks. You reminded me that not every battle is mine to fight. That moment taught me something valuable, and I am grateful.

Carry that same wisdom into your marriage. Not every irritation or disagreement is worth turning into a fight. Some things are better overlooked for the sake of peace. Learn to pause, pray, and discern if the issue is truly worth addressing or if love can simply cover it.

Tips:

1. Pause before responding to irritations.
2. Ask yourself, *Will this matter in a year?* before raising the issue.
3. Address only what truly threatens unity, values, or God's principles.

Red Flags:

1. Responding with intense emotions to minor issues can indicate a tendency to escalate conflicts rather than resolve them.

2. Focusing on small flaws or mistakes, rather than the bigger picture, may lead to unnecessary tension in a relationship.

3. Failing to consider the context or circumstances surrounding an issue can result in fighting over misunderstandings.

Reflection:

1. Do you sometimes insist on "winning" small arguments instead of letting them go?

2. How can you better pause and discern before responding in moments of irritation?

3. What small issues in marriage might you need to release to God instead of fighting over?

Prayer:

Father, give Dey the wisdom to know which battles are worth fighting and the patience to let go of the rest. Teach her to overlook offenses with grace and to preserve peace in her marriage. May she reflect Your love in the way she handles disagreements. In Jesus Christ's name. Amen.

13

Don't Compare Him to Anyone Else

Each one should test their own actions. Then
they can take pride in themselves alone, without comparing themselves to someone else.
(Galatians 6:4 NIV)

Insight

Comparisons create insecurity and resentment, but celebrating uniqueness builds confidence and intimacy.

Tamilore, I want to revisit something from earlier in this letter. When you were about twelve years old, you looked at me one day and said with confidence, "Dad, you can't replace me." You said it emphatically, as if you knew beyond a doubt who you were, your value, and your worth. That confidence blessed me deeply. Not everyone is fortunate enough to grow up with that sense of identity, but you have always known how precious and irreplaceable you are.

From the time you began walking at just eight months old without even crawling, you have been uniquely distinguished. You are fearfully and wonderfully made—and Jeremiah is too. Part of your calling in marriage will be to remind him of his own worth when the world makes him doubt it.

To that extent, do not compare him to me, to your brother, or to anyone else. Comparisons can slowly poison a relationship. They make people feel inadequate and unloved. I know you wouldn't naturally do this, but I want to repeat it here as a reminder: Your husband is uniquely made by God, and he deserves to be loved and celebrated for himself.

Tips:

1. Celebrate his unique strengths and accomplishments, even if they look different from yours.

2. Guard your heart against "social media envy" or unrealistic standards.

3. Speak words that affirm his individuality and God-given purpose.

Red Flags:

1. Regularly seeking opinions from friends or family about your partner may indicate doubts about your relationship.

2. Frequently idealizing the relationships or qualities of others may suggest dissatisfaction with Jeremiah and a focus on what you perceive to be missing.

Reflection:

1. Do you ever compare Jeremiah—silently or out loud—to others in ways that could hurt him?

2. What unique qualities has God given him that you can celebrate today?

3. How can you remind him of his worth when he struggles with self-doubt?

Prayer:

Father, help Dey to honor her husband as the unique man You created him to be. Teach her to resist the temptation to compare, and instead, to celebrate his strengths and gifts. May her words and actions affirm his worth and reflect Your love. In Jesus Christ's name. Amen.

Part Four:

Understanding and Supporting Him

14

You Can't Change Him—Trust God to Work in Him

He who began a good work in you will carry it
on to completion until the day of Christ Jesus.
(Philippians 1:6 NIV)

Insight

Acceptance fosters security, but attempts to "fix" another person create resistance.

Beautiful one, if I had a dollar for every woman who confidently told me she could change a man, I would be a millionaire by now. This reflects the God-given creativity and determination that so many women carry. Often, wives see their husband as a "project." *Just give me enough time and effort, and I'll shape him into what he needs to be!*

But Dey, you and I have spoken about this many times—only God can truly change a person. He is the

Creator, and He works through circumstances, challenges, and experiences to shape hearts. Yet, even God does not force us; He respects the free will He gave us.

For most men, what you see is what you get. Jeremiah may grow, but not because you pressure him. He will grow in response to God's work in his heart, your love, and the environment of trust and respect you create. Remember, nagging, pushing, or criticizing rarely lead to change. But prayer, patience, and encouragement are far more powerful.

So, don't carry the heavy burden of "fixing" him. That is not your role. Instead, pray for him, believe in him, and trust that God who began a good work in him will be faithful to complete it.

Tips:

1. Pray instead of pressuring.

2. Celebrate small signs of growth.

3. Remember that God is the ultimate transformer of hearts.

Red Flags:

1. If you are beginning to feel responsible for his growth and believe that it's your duty to fix or improve his character, this may reflect a lack of faith in God's ability to work in his life.

2. Neglecting your own growth and focusing exclusively on changing your husband may lead you to overlook your own personal and spiritual development.

Reflection:

1. When you release the pressure to change Jeremiah, you free both yourself and him. Acceptance creates safety, and safety creates space for growth. True transformation is never your burden; it belongs to God.

Prayer:

Father, help Dey to love and accept her husband as he is, trusting You to do the work in him that she cannot. Teach her patience, fill her with grace, and remind her daily that only You can truly transform a heart. In Jesus Christ's name. Amen.

15

Give Him Space When He Needs It

There is a time for everything, and a season for every activity under the heavens.
(Ecclesiastes 3:1 NIV)

Insight

A healthy marriage balances autonomy and intimacy, creating secure attachment.

Alake, God gave Adam work in the garden of Eden before giving him Eve as a helper. Adam spent time alone and became accustomed to solitude. It is no surprise then that many men still need space—moments to recharge, reflect, or figure things out.

Women, on the other hand, are often more relational and naturally inclined toward nurturing connection. You've probably heard terms like *dependency, codependency,* and *interdependency.* The healthiest marriages are built on interdependency—where both partners support each other without losing themselves.

Alake, you have always been remarkably independent. You walked at eight months old without crawling. You skipped the bottle, moving straight from nursing to solid foods. You excelled in school, making high honor rolls with little assistance. You found your own college—Indiana Wesleyan University—without relying on us. You've traveled widely, driven across the West Coast during COVID, explored Asia, and visited forty-nine out of fifty U.S. states.

Independence has always been your strength. But marriage invites you into a new rhythm—interdependence with Jeremiah. That means sometimes giving him space when he needs it and knowing he will do the same for you. I trust that your independence, paired with your maturity, will make this balance natural for you.

Tips:

1. Let him recharge without guilt.

2. Use that time to nurture your own soul.

3. Trust that space makes room for deeper connection.

Red Flags:

1. Filling your agenda with joint activities, and not allowing for individual time, can lead to feelings of overwhelm.

2. Failing to recognize when he needs time for himself, especially if he seems tired or withdrawn, indicates a lack of awareness of his needs.

Reflection:

1. Allowing Jeremiah space is not rejection—it is respect. It means you honor how God designed him. And while he regroups, you can deepen your own walk with God and grow as an individual, which, in turn, strengthens your marriage.

Prayer:

Father, give Dey wisdom to honor her husband's need for space. Help her to use that time, not for worry, but for growth, prayer, and joy. May her marriage reflect both freedom and closeness rooted in Your love. In Jesus Christ's name. Amen.

16

Honor His Journey—Help without Pushing

As iron sharpens iron, so one person sharpens
another. (Proverbs 27:17 NIV)

It [love] always protects, always trusts,
always hopes, always perseveres.
(1 Corinthians 13:7 NIV)

Insight

True help empowers without control. Respecting his process builds trust and unity.

Dey, I'll never forget the ACT story. You were already excelling—acing it multiple times—yet I kept encouraging (pushing really) you to take it again and again. After the third attempt, you looked at me and said firmly, "Dad, I'm not doing this anymore." That moment was humbling for me. I thought I was helping, but in reality, I was projecting my own experiences, fears, and values onto you. I wasn't empowering you; I was pressuring you. That is one of my regrets.

What I learned from that experience is that helping someone doesn't always mean pushing them. In fact, pushing often has the opposite effect—it can create resistance, resentment, or exhaustion. Encouragement is powerful, but it must be rooted in love and respect, not in control.

Now, as you walk into marriage, remember this lesson. You and Jeremiah are uniquely created by God. Even though you and I are a lot alike in many ways, we also have distinct differences, and that is beautiful. In the same way, Jeremiah's journey will not always match yours. He has his own path, his own process, and his own timeline. Your role is not to push him into becoming who you think he should be, but to lovingly encourage him to become the man God is shaping him to be.

Honor his journey. Respect his seasons of growth. Just as God has been patient with you in your development, be patient with him. Some stages will feel fast, some will feel slow, and some may not make sense to you—but trust that God is at work in both of you. Marriage is not about remaking each other into your own image—it is about growing together into Christ's image.

When you choose empathy over pressure and encouragement over control, you create an environment in which Jeremiah will feel safe to grow, stumble, and rise again. That kind of love not only builds connection but also reflects the heart of Christ.

Tips:

1. Instead of pushing, ask, "How can I support you?"

2. Offer suggestions, not ultimatums.

3. Listen carefully to his dreams and fears.

4. Trust that God is guiding his growth, even when it doesn't match your expectations.

Red Flags:

1. A lack of enthusiasm for shared activities or conversations can indicate that he feels overwhelmed or pressured.

2. Defensiveness during discussions about expectations or responsibilities may be a sign that he feels cornered.

3. If he starts avoiding certain topics or conversations altogether, it may indicate a reluctance to engage due to feeling pushed.

Reflection:

Pushing can break trust, but patient encouragement builds it. Respecting Jeremiah's journey honors not only him but also God who is writing his story. You are not the author of his life—God is. Your privilege is to walk beside him as his partner offering love, faith, and gentle support.

Prayer:

Father, teach Dey to encourage her husband without controlling him. Help her to respect his journey, trust Your timing, and see him through Your eyes. Give her patience, wisdom, and the humility to walk with him in love so that together they may reflect Your kingdom. In Jesus Christ's name. Amen.

17

The Stages of Marriage— Growing through Each Season

Two are better than one. (Ecclesiastes 4:9a)

Insight

Marital contentment looks different in each season. Appreciate the blessings of every stage, even when it doesn't feel like summer.

Deyo, this is something I wish someone had told me before I got married. At the beginning, I truly thought marriage would always feel like summer—warm, bright, and filled with joy. But I have since learned that marriage, like life itself, has seasons: summer, fall, winter, and spring. Each season carries its own beauty, challenges, and opportunities for growth.

What matters is learning to anticipate and recognize which season you are in. Being proactive rather than reactive makes all the difference.

Think of our lake house: In the summer, the sunsets are stunning and the water feels alive. In the fall, the leaves change colors, reminding us that endings can be just as beautiful as beginnings. Winter covers the lake with snow, bringing stillness and reflection, while spring revives everything with new growth, fresh leaves, and hope.

Marriage is just like that. Each season has its own uniqueness. Some seasons will feel light and joyful; others may feel heavy or uncertain. But every season carries its own kind of beauty if you are willing to look for it.

Tips:

1. Normalize challenges as part of growth.
2. Adjust expectations as you move through different stages of life together.
3. Remember, seasons change, and no season lasts forever.

Red Flags:

1. Believing a difficult season will never end and losing hope
2. Comparing your marriage season to someone else's and feeling resentful
3. Refusing to adapt or grow when life's circumstances shift

4. Pulling away from each other during winter seasons instead of leaning closer

Reflection:

1. Dey and Jeremiah, congratulations on this exciting new chapter in your life! As you embrace the early stage of your marriage, filled with romance and new experiences, remember that you'll also face daily challenges. Open communication and patience will be key as you navigate this journey together. Embrace each stage you encounter, as it will deepen your bond and enrich your partnership. How can you support each other as you adjust to these changes?

Prayer:

Father, teach Dey and Jeremiah to recognize and embrace every season of their marriage. Give them patience in the winters, gratitude in the summers, courage in the falls, and renewal in the springs. May they never lose sight of the beauty You place in each stage of life, and may they walk together, hand in hand, trusting that with You, every season has purpose. In Jesus Christ's name. Amen.

18

The Gift of Fun and Playfulness in Marriage

Your love is more delightful than wine.
(Song of Solomon 1:2b NIV)

Insight

Play and novelty release dopamine, deepening joy and sustaining attraction.

I once counseled a couple who were constantly stressed by work and parenting responsibilities. Arguments became their daily language, and the home felt heavy. At one point, I taught them what you taught me and encouraged them to bring back playfulness—something as simple as a weekly game night, surprising each other with inside jokes, or spontaneous outings. Within weeks, they noticed something change: Laughter returned. Conflicts softened. They started to remember why they fell in love in the first place. That is the power of joy and play—it doesn't erase problems, but it creates space for love to breathe again.

Dr. Dey, you are one fun-loving, adventurous, creative, and intelligent princess! Since you were young, you have brought sunshine, joy, and creativity into our lives and into the lives of everyone you meet.

Let me jog your memory: the UKA card you made, the charades during Thanksgiving, the surprise tickets to the jazz festival, our walks down the beach in Waikiki, and so many other moments. I used to be stiff and serious, but you brought playfulness into my life and showed me that it's okay not to always be so serious.

This is who you are—sunlight and joy. Please never lose that. Keep smiling, keep having fun, and keep being the sunshine you are to Jeremiah. Your ability to create fun and laughter will help sustain love through the years.

Tips:

1. Plan regular date nights, no matter how busy life gets.

2. Surprise him with small, playful gestures.

3. Bring humor into everyday life—it lightens even heavy seasons.

Red Flags:

1. Allowing stress and busyness to steal all joy and play
2. Losing sight of fun after children or responsibilities enter the picture
3. Believing playfulness is "childish" rather than a gift
4. Neglecting novelty and falling into stale routines

Reflection:

1. Joy in marriage is not accidental; it's cultivated.
2. Playfulness strengthens intimacy and keeps romance alive.
3. Shared laughter can diffuse conflict and create bonding memories.

Prayer:

Father, thank You for the gift of joy and laughter. Teach Dey and Jeremiah to cherish the playful spirit that keeps marriage alive and vibrant. Help them not to be weighed down by life's responsibilities to the point of losing joy. May their home be filled with smiles, surprises, and the kind of fun that reflects Your goodness and love. In Jesus Christ's name. Amen.

19

Gratitude as a Daily Practice

Give thanks in all circumstances.
(1 Thessalonians 5:18a NIV)

Insight

Gratitude strengthens positivity, resilience, and satisfaction in marriage.

I once knew a couple who went through financial struggles that put incredible strain on their marriage. At first, all they could see were the bills and the stress. But they decided to start a "gratitude jar," writing one thing they were thankful for each day. Weeks later, when they looked back, they realized that God had been faithful in countless small ways—through friends' generosity, through health, and through opportunities to work together. Gratitude shifted their perspective, helped them endure the hard season, and drew them closer instead of driving them apart.

Sunshine, when someone gives you something, you usually write a lengthy, heartfelt thank-you note—you don't just send a quick text. I remember when you came back from a vacation a few years ago. You looked at me and your mom and said, "Thank you for taking care of me, and thank you for appreciating me and making me feel valued." We were just doing our job as parents, but your spirit of honor and gratitude made us feel deeply appreciated.

So, it feels almost strange to give you advice here because you already exemplify what it means to live with gratitude. Still, I want to encourage you to keep your heart open to appreciation—not only toward us, but especially toward Jeremiah and toward the Lord. Write down your blessings, big and small. Remind yourself and Jeremiah daily of God's goodness. Gratitude doesn't just honor others; it strengthens joy in marriage.

Tips:

1. Share one thing you are grateful for each night before bed.

2. Keep a couple's gratitude journal, and review it regularly.

3. Thank each other not only for big things, but also for daily faithfulness.

Red Flags:

1. Taking daily acts of love for granted
2. Focusing on what is missing instead of appreciating what is present
3. Using comparison to fuel discontent
4. Forgetting to thank God in difficult seasons

Reflection:

1. Gratitude is a habit that keeps the heart soft and open.
2. It transforms ordinary moments into sacred ones.
3. A grateful heart sees blessings where others only see burdens.

Prayer:

Father, help Dey and Jeremiah to live with a grateful heart. Teach them to see Your blessings in every season of life and to appreciate each other daily. Protect them from discontentment and complaining, and instead, fill their home with thankfulness and joy. May gratitude always be the language of their marriage. In Jesus Christ's name. Amen.

20

Building a Legacy Together

As for me and my house, we will serve the
LORD. (Joshua 24:15b)

Insight

Shared purpose sustains long-term fulfillment in marriage.

I once knew a couple who came from very different backgrounds. The husband's family was wealthy but spiritually shallow; the wife's family was deeply faithful but struggled financially. They made a decision early in marriage that their legacy would combine the best of both—financial wisdom and strong faith. They committed to tithing, raising their children in the church, and using their home for hospitality. Years later, their children not only excelled academically and professionally but also carried deep faith in Christ. Their intentional choice to build a legacy together changed their family's story for generations.

Dear Dey

Adeyoola Ajibola Oluwatamilore Alake omo Alao, I want to remind you of who you are.

Your father is an elder at Abundant Life Church, who gave his life to Christ at the age of ten years old. Your mother is a prayer warrior who, to the surprise of many, was ordained a deaconess and was later elevated by God to serve as an elder.

Your grandfather (my dad) was a school principal who touched countless lives and was honored as the *Asiwaju* of Ejigbo—a title meaning "the one in front," conferred by the king. You come from a royal line, which is why your name begins with *Ade*—meaning "crown." Every one of your siblings and cousins carries that mark of royalty. Adeyoola means *Crown of Joy*, and it is no coincidence that you are a leader full of the joy of the Lord.

Your great-grandfather, Papa Alao, was a Baptist minister so faithful that a street in Atakpamé, Togo still bears his name. You were also named after your grandmother, a school principal who was passionate for Jesus and known for her radical generosity, sowing seeds in secret that blessed many. Her mother, Mama Iwo, was one of the first nurses in Africa to open her own practice and employ doctors. She raised eight remarkable children while also serving as a deaconess.

On your mother's side, your grandfather, Archdeacon John Olaniyi Ojo, was a school principal, Archdeacon, and Venerable in the Anglican Church of Nigeria. He built two schools from the ground up. His wife, Grandma Ojo (née Fearon), was an accomplished home economics teacher, the daughter of a minister, and the granddaughter of one of the earliest Christians martyred for preaching the gospel.

So, Dey, you see that you have inherited a rich Christian heritage of faith, education, service, and leadership. This is the legacy that has been handed to you. The question now is: What legacy will you and Jeremiah build together?

We prayed for children who would surpass us in every way, and that is my prayer for you, Dr. Adeyoola Ajibola Tamilore Mojoyinola Alake omo Alao—that your legacy will outshine ours and glorify God.

Tips:

1. Discuss the kind of legacy you want to leave—spiritual, relational, and practical.

2. Serve together in ministry, your community, and your family.

3. Be intentional about modeling faith and love for the next generation.

Red Flags:

1. Living only for personal comfort without thinking generationally

2. Serving separately without aligning as a couple

3. Allowing culture or money to define your legacy instead of faith

4. Neglecting to pass down spiritual values to your children

Reflection:

1. Legacy is not built in a day; it is the fruit of consistent choices.

2. A marriage with a shared mission can withstand storms.

3. What you cultivate in private will ripple into public in future generations.

Prayer:

Father, thank You for the rich heritage of faith that Dey and Jeremiah carry. Help them to honor the legacy of those before them while also building something new and beautiful for those who will come after them. Give them wisdom to serve You faithfully, courage to lead their family well, and a vision for a legacy that will glorify Your name. May their children and grandchildren rise up and call them blessed. In Jesus Christ's name. Amen.

A Final Word of Advice

As you embark on this lifelong journey, know that marriage is not a sprint but a marathon. There will be days of laughter and days of tears, moments of clarity and seasons of confusion. Yet, through it all, God remains faithful, and His Word will always light your path.

The principles in these pages are not meant to burden you but to bless you. You will not live them out perfectly—no one does. But if you keep returning to God, keep growing in grace, and keep choosing love, you will discover the beauty of a marriage that deepens with time.

Always remember that your marriage is bigger than the two of you. It is a reflection of Christ and His Church, a living testimony of God's covenant love. Your union is not only for your joy but also for His glory.

My prayer is that you and your husband will not only build a strong marriage but also a legacy—one that blesses your children, your community, and generations to come.

Dear Dey

I love you more than words can say, and I will continue to pray for you both, always.

With love, pride, and blessing,

Dad

Meet the Author

Kola Alao, MD is a psychiatrist who lives and works in New York State. Growing up in Western Nigeria, he first moved to the United Kingdom, and then the United States, for advanced medical training. Experience as an immigrant has given him fresh insights on human behavior. Teaching medical students and residents has further expanded his familiarity with motivation and the drive for achievement. Dr. Alao writes from a deep understanding of human psychology combined with years of thorough, genuine self-reflection.

Dedicated to living his values as a Christian, husband, father, and medical doctor, he always sees the good in other people, turning a compassionate eye on each person's effort to improve themselves, encouraging everyone to make positive changes that align with their values, behaviors, and aspirations. Introducing tried-and-true methods to track the habits and character flaws that hold people back, Dr. Alao asks his readers to look deep within and offers his help.

With years of experience practicing a variety of therapeutic methods, Dr. Alao and his wife, a psychiatric nurse practitioner, have developed helpful treatments for depression, post-traumatic stress disorder, obsessive compulsive behaviors, and substance abuse disorders utilizing transcranial magnetic stimulation (TMS). They are active in their church and also spend considerable time each year volunteering in several African countries.

In this book, Dr. Alao shares his insights and wisdom with those who seek to build successful lives, offering good advice to help us make meaningful contributions to our communities and the wider world.

Dr. Kola Alao can be contacted at 360favor@gmail.com or by visiting www.tmspsychiatry.org.

What I Wish I'd Learned

In *What I Wish I'd Learned*, Dr. Alao—renowned psychiatrist and mentor—offers a roadmap for anyone ready to take charge of their life's direction. Structured into three essential pillars—Personal Development, Professional Growth, and Living a Balanced Life—this book is a toolkit for achieving genuine self-improvement and fulfillment.

Packed with relatable stories, psychological insights, and practical exercises, *What I Wish I'd Learned* will empower you to strengthen the foundations of your personal and professional life. Whether you're at the start of your journey or seeking a fresh perspective, Dr. Alao's compassionate wisdom will inspire you to live a life of greater depth, balance, and purpose.